Life Processes

CLASSIFICATION

Revised and Updated

Holly Wallace

Heinemann Library
Chicago, Illinois

Customer Service 888-454-2279
Visit our website at www.heinemannraintree.com

Designed by David Poole and Kamae Design
Printed in China by WKT Company Limited

10 09 08 07 06
10 9 8 7 6 5 4 3 2 1

New edition ISBN:1-4034-8845-2 (hardcover)
              1-4034-8852-5 (paperback)

The Library of Congress has cataloged the first edition as follows:

Wallace, Holly, 1961- .
        Classification / Holly Wallace.
              p. cm. -- (Life processes)
        Includes bibliographical references (p.)
        ISBN 1-57572-337-9 (library)
        1. Biology -- Classificatin -- Juvenile literature. [1. Biology--Classification.] I. Title. II. Series.
QH38 .G26 2000
570.1'2--dc21
                          00-040974

Acknowledgements
The publishers would like to thank the following for permission to reproduce photographs:
Bruce Coleman: Hans Reinhard p.**24**; Mary Evans Picture Library: p.**4**; NHPA: Martin Harvey pp.**5**, **29**, Laurie Campbell pp.**6**, **9**, MI Walker p.**6**, Andy Rouse p.**7**, ANT pp.**8**, **23**, Stephen Dalton pp.**8**, **16**, **20**, **28**, Alberto Nardi p.**10**, EA Janes p.**11**, Daniel Zupanc p.**12**, Anthony Bannister pp.**13**, **15**, **28**, NA Callow p.**14**, GI Bernard p.**16**, John Shaw p.**17**, Norbert Wu p.**18**, Daniel Heuclin pp.**19**, **22**, **25**, LUTRA p.**21**, Christophe Ratier p.**25**, Nigel J Dennis p.**27**; Photodisc: p.**7**, p.**26**.

Cover photograph of a Christmas cactus reproduced with permission of FLPA Images/Holt Studios.

The publishers would like to thank Mary Jones for her assistance in the preparation of this book.

Disclaimer
All the Internet addresses (URLs) given in this book were valid at the time of going to press. However, due to the dynamic nature of the Internet, some addresses may have changed, or sites may have changed or ceased to exist since publication. While the author and publishers regret any inconvenience this may cause readers, no responsibility for any such changes can be accepted by either the author or the publishers.

The paper used to print this book comes from sustainable resources.

CONTENTS

Any words appearing in the text in bold, **like this**, are explained in the glossary.

WHAT IS CLASSIFICATION?

There is an amazing number of living things on Earth. Scientists use the word **organism** to describe anything that is alive. However, they also need a way of identifying individual **species** from among the millions that exist. To do this, they divide living things into groups. This is called classification, or **taxonomy**. It is similar to the system used in a library where each book is given a code or number to make it easier to find.

LINNAEUS'S SYSTEM

The modern system of classification was devised by the Swedish scientist, Carl von Linné (1707–1778). He gave each known living thing a two-part **Latin** name. For example, a tiger is *Panthera tigris*. The two parts work like your family name and given name, showing which family the organism belongs to and identifying it as an individual. Latin was used so that the name was the same all over the world and could be understood by everyone. Von Linné even Latinized his own name to Carolus Linnaeus. Today, we still use Latin and Latin-like names. For example, the name of the scientist who discovered a new species is often Latinized and used as part of the name of the species.

▲ Carl von Linné.

COMMON AND SCIENTIFIC NAMES

Many living things have a common name as well as a scientific (Latin) name. However, the same common name might refer to several different animals. For example, you find badgers in Europe and in the United States but they are not the same animal. Using their scientific names, *Meles meles* (European badger) and *Taxidea taxus* (American badger), avoids any confusion.

HOW DOES CLASSIFICATION WORK?

Scientists divide living things into groups, depending on the features that they have in common. You can see the main groups below.

- Kingdoms: These are the largest groups. They include the animal kingdom and the plant kingdom.
- Phyla (singular: phylum): Similar classes of living things are grouped into phyla.
- Classes: Similar orders are grouped into classes.
- Orders: Similar families are grouped into orders.
- Families: Related genera are grouped into families.
- Genera (singular: genus): Similar species are grouped into genera. They all have similar features.
- Species: These are the smallest groups. Members of a species can breed together to produce young.

TIGER CLASSIFICATION TABLE

This table shows how classification works for one species, the tiger (*Panthera tigris*).

Kingdom:	Animalia (animals)
Phylum:	Chordata (**chordates**)
Sub-phylum:	Vertebrata (**vertebrates**—have backbones)
Class:	Mammalia (mammals)
Order:	Carnivora (carnivores— eat only meat)
Family:	Felidae (cats)
Genus:	*Panthera*
Species:	*tigris*

▲ *Panthera tigris* is the scientific name for the tiger.

DID YOU KNOW ?

Scientists have no real idea how many species of living things exist on Earth. About 2 million have been described and classified but the actual number may be 10 times higher. New species of plants and animals are being discovered every year.

FIVE KINGDOMS

The largest group of classification is the kingdom. At one time, scientists only recognized two kingdoms of living things—the plant kingdom and the animal kingdom. However, many organisms do not fit into these two groups. They are neither plants nor animals, or they have features of both. Today, we divide living things into five kingdoms.

PROKARYOTA KINGDOM

Prokaryotas are tiny, single-celled organisms such as bacteria and blue-green **algae**. They are believed to be one of the most ancient forms of life on Earth. Their cells are very simple and, unlike all other living things, do not have a **nucleus**. More than 3,000 species of prokaryotas are known, but many scientists think there may be hundreds of thousands of them.

PROTIST KINGDOM

The protist kingdom is made up mostly of organisms that have a single cell with a nucleus. For example, an amoeba is a protist. There are more than 28,000 known species of protists. All protists live in damp places or in water.

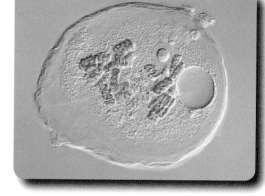

▲ An amoeba is a protist.

FUNGI KINGDOM

Fungi are organisms such as molds, mushrooms, and mildew. The body of a fungus is made up of a network of threads called fungus cells. Unlike plant cells, fungus cells do not contain **chlorophyll** and cannot make their own food by **photosynthesis**. Instead, fungi feed by absorbing food from other organisms, both alive and dead. There are about 75,000 known fungi species.

► Fly agaric (*Amanita muscaria*) is a highly poisonous fungus.

PLANT KINGDOM

Plant cells have rigid cell walls made of **cellulose**. Their cells contain a green substance called chlorophyll, which they use to make their own food by photosynthesis. For this they need water, carbon dioxide, and sunlight. Plants do not move from place to place. There are more than 400,000 known plant species.

ANIMAL KINGDOM

Animals are made up of many cells that form specialized **tissues**, **organs**, and **organ systems**. Animal cells do not have rigid walls, and they cannot make their own food. Most animals have to move around to find food and escape from danger. There are about 1.5 million known species of animals.

USING A KEY

You can determine the identity of an organism by using a key, like the very simple one below for big cats. A key is a set of questions and each answer leads to another question. This continues until you find the name of the organism.

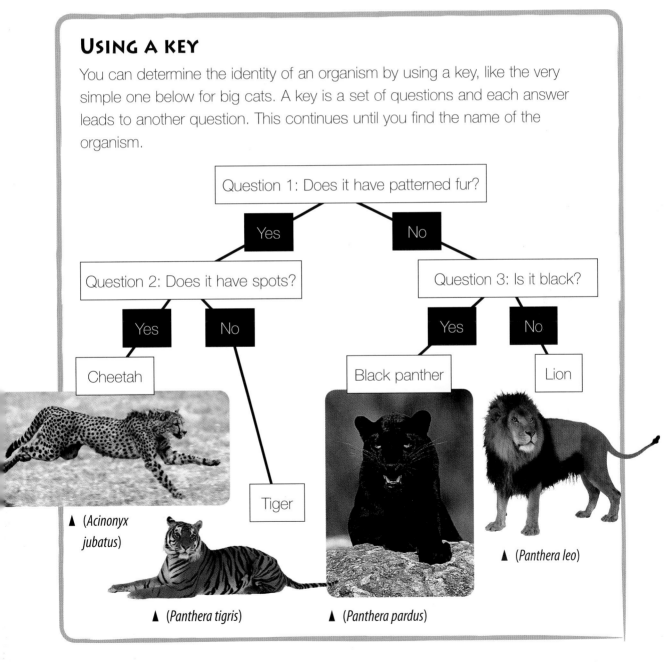

Question 1: Does it have patterned fur?

Yes / No

Question 2: Does it have spots?

Yes / No

Cheetah

Question 3: Is it black?

Yes / No

Black panther / Lion

Tiger

▲ (*Acinonyx jubatus*)

▲ (*Panthera tigris*)

▲ (*Panthera pardus*)

▲ (*Panthera leo*)

PLANTS WITHOUT FLOWERS

The plant kingdom is divided into flowering plants and plants that do not produce flowers. Plants without flowers have been growing on Earth for 300 million years. The prehistoric ancestors of modern horsetails and club mosses grew up to 100 feet (30 meters) tall, much higher than a house. Most non-flowering plants grow from tiny, dust-like specks called **spores**. The spores are made and released in the thousands, then carried away by the wind. If they land in a suitable place, they grow into new plants.

▼ Giant bull kelp seaweed (*Durvillea antarctica*).

ALGAE

Algae are very simple, non-flowering plants, with no real roots, leaves, or stems. They usually grow in water and range in size from microscopic, single-celled plants to gigantic seaweeds. They are classified according to their color—red, green, or brown. Plants give off oxygen as waste when they photosynthesize. Sea algae produce about 80 percent of all the oxygen in the air. Some biologists classify all types of algae as protists (see page 6).

MOSSES AND LIVERWORTS

Mosses and liverworts are mainly small, ground-hugging plants that live in damp places. They do not have flowers but produce their spores in a small capsule that is held up on a tiny stalk. When the capsule opens, the spores are carried away on the wind.

◀ A spore capsule of a star moss (*Polytrichum* species) ready to release the spores into the air.

FERNS, HORSETAILS, AND CLUB MOSSES

Ferns, horsetails, and club mosses also grow from spores. Ferns are plants with frond-like leaves that grow from underground stems. Some have rusty spots under their leaves. These are spore-bearing structures called sporangia.

▼ A monkey puzzle tree (*Araucaria araucana*).

CONIFERS

Conifers (class *Gymnospermae*) are trees such as pines, larches, and redwoods. Unlike the other non-flowering plants, they grow new plants from seeds, formed when male **pollen** joins with female **ovules**. They do not produce flowers. Instead, their pollen, ovules, and seeds grow in woody cones. There are roughly 550 species of conifer.

DID YOU KNOW ?

Lichens are a mixture of a fungus and an alga. The alga provides the fungus with food made by photosynthesis. In turn, the fungus protects the alga and provides it with water. It is a highly successful combination. Lichens are extremely hardy and can survive in very cold or hostile conditions.

Simple plants		Ferns and horsetails		Conifers	
Kingdom:	Plantae (plants)	Kingdom:	Plantae (plants)	Kingdom:	Plantae (plants)
Phylum:	Bryophyta (plants with simple roots, stems, and leaves but no vascular tissue)	Phyla:	Filicinophyta (ferns); Sphenophyta (horsetails); Lycophyta (club mosses)	Phyla:	Coniferophyta (conifers); Cycadophyta (cycads); Ginkophyta (ginkgoes); Gnetophyta (gnetophytes—tropical and desert shrubs)
Classes:	Hepaticae (liverworts); Musci (mosses); Anthocerotae (hornworts)				

FLOWERING PLANTS

Flowering plants belong to the phylum Angiospermae. Flowers contain the plant's male and female parts, which are needed to make seeds that will grow into new plants. Some flowers have both male and female parts in the same flower, others are either male or female. The male parts make a fine powder called pollen. For a seed to grow, the pollen must join with a female ovule. Pollen is often carried from flower to flower by the wind or by animals. This is called **pollination**. Flowering plants are by far the biggest group of plants with about 250,000 species. They first grew on Earth roughly 100 million years ago.

MONOCOTYLEDONS

Flowering plants can be divided into two classes, monocotyledons and dicotyledons. A cotyledon is a tiny leaf inside a seed. Until the new plant grows its first leaves, it lives off food stored in the cotyledon. Monocotyledons have only one of these leaves in their seeds. Other features include narrow leaves with parallel **veins** and usually three parts to their flowers. Irises, daffodils, and grasses are monocotyledons.

▲ A field of poppies (*Papaver* species). Poppies are dicotyledons.

DICOTYLEDONS

Dicotyledons have two cotyledons in their seeds. They include plants such as daisies, carrots, cabbages, oak trees, cacti, and roses. Most have broad leaves with a branching pattern of veins. Their flowers are usually divided into four or five parts.

Most types of plants are called vascular plants. This means that they have a system of tiny tubes running through their stems. These tubes are called **vascular tissue** and there are two types called xylem and phloem. The xylem carry water from the roots up through the plant. The phloem carry the sugary food made in the leaves to all parts of the plant. Some simple, non-flowering plants, such as algae, mosses, and liverworts, do not have vascular tissue.

TREES

Trees are plants with tall, woody trunks instead of stems. The two most common groups of trees are conifers (see page 9) and broad-leaved trees. Conifers make seeds but do not make flowers. Broad-leaved trees are flowering plants. For example, cherry trees belong to the rose family. Many broad-leaved trees are **deciduous**. This means that they lose their leaves once a year.

▲ A beech tree (*Fagus sylvatica*) in fall. Beeches are deciduous.

Flowering plant classification

Kingdom:	Plantae (plants)
Phylum:	Angiospermophyta (angiosperms, or plants with flowers and fruits)
Classes:	Monocotyledonae (monocotyledons, e.g.: daffodils, grasses) Dicotyledonae (dicotyledons, e.g.: oak trees, roses)
Number of species:	more than 250,000

INVERTEBRATES

Invertebrates are animals that do not have **vertebrae** (backbones) or hard skeletons inside their bodies. With some 950,000 species, there are far more invertebrates than vertebrates. About 97 percent of animal species are invertebrates. They are divided into many different groups, including insects (see page 14), mollusks, worms, starfish, and jellyfish.

▲ An edible snail (*Helix pomatia*).

MOLLUSKS

After insects, mollusks make up the second largest group of invertebrates. All mollusks have a soft body that is often protected by a hard shell. Most live in water. Mollusks include snails and slugs (class *Gastropoda*); clams and mussels (class *Bivalvia*); and octopuses and squid (class *Cephalopoda*). Bivalves have two parts to their shells. Cephalopods have a small shell hidden inside their bodies.

JELLYFISH AND SEA ANEMONES

Jellyfish, sea anemones, and corals belong to a group of invertebrates called cnidarians (phylum *Cnidaria*). They have soft, circular bodies and mouths surrounded by stinging tentacles used for catching **prey**. All jellyfish can sting, but the box jellyfish (*Chironex fleckeri*) of Australia is deadly. Its poison can kill a person within four minutes of being stung.

WORMS

Many worms, such as earthworms, leeches, and lugworms, are annelids (phylum *Annelida*). They have long, tubular bodies divided into segments. The longest earthworm is the giant *Michrochaetus rappi* from South Africa, which grows over three feet long. Earthworms spend most of their lives underground. Their burrows help to keep the soil healthy by allowing air and water to circulate.

"SPINY-SKINNED"

Starfish, sea urchins, and their relatives are echinoderms (phylum *Echinodermata*). Their name means "spiny-skinned." Echinoderms have chalky skeletons and bodies arranged in five parts. Many starfish, for example, have five arms. If a starfish loses an arm, it can grow another one. Underneath each arm are rows of **tube feet** that the starfish uses to move and also to grip its prey.

▲ Two echinoderms—a starfish and a sea-urchin.

Invertebrate classification	
Kingdom:	Animalia (animals)
Major phyla:	1. Cnidaria (coelenterates)
	2. Ctenophora (comb jellies)
	3. Platyhelminthes (flatworms)
	4. Nematoda (roundworms)
	5. Mollusca (mollusks)
	6. Annelida (segmented worms)
	7. Arthropoda (arthropods)

Mollusk classification	
Kingdom:	Animalia (animals)
Phylum:	Mollusca (mollusks)
Classes:	1. Polyplacophora (chitons)
	2. Gastropoda (snails, slugs)
	3. Bivalvia (clams, mussels)
	4. Cephalopoda (squid, octopuses)
	(plus 3 minor classes)
Number of orders:	about 45
Number of species:	about 75,000

ARTHROPODS

The biggest group of invertebrates is the arthropods (phylum Arthropoda). It includes insects, arachnids (see pages 16–17), crustaceans, centipedes, and millipedes. With more than 1 million known species, it is the largest group of animals on Earth. All arthropods have bodies divided into segments and legs that bend at joints. Their soft bodies are covered with hard cases or shells called **exoskeletons**. Most anthropods have two **antennae**.

INSECT IDENTIFICATION

Insects (class *Insecta*) live all over the world in all climates. All insects have three parts to their bodies—the head, **thorax**, and **abdomen**. They have six pairs of legs attached to their thorax. Most insects have two pairs of wings and can fly. Flies have only one pair of wings. Adult ants and aphids have none. Insects have **compound eyes** made up of hundreds of tiny lenses and one pair of antennae for smelling, tasting, touching, and sensing vibrations in the air.

Insect classification	
Kingdom:	Animalia (animals)
Phylum:	Arthropoda (arthropods)
Class:	Insecta (insects)
Number of orders:	19
Number of species:	about 1 million

► Honeybees (*Apis mellifera*) are typical insects.

CRUSTACEANS

Like insects, crustaceans (class *Crustacea*) are arthropods. Most of the 44,000 species of crustaceans live in the sea. Woodlice are unusual because they live on land. Crustaceans have bodies divided into many segments, each with a pair of jointed legs for walking and swimming. They have two pairs of antennae, and most are covered in hard shells. Crustaceans include crabs, lobsters, barnacles, water fleas, shrimp, and woodlice.

CENTIPEDES AND MILLIPEDES

Centipedes and millipedes are myriapods, or "many-legged," arthropods. Both have long, many-segmented bodies and, from a distance, look quite alike. However, centipedes have one pair of legs on each body segment while millipedes have two. Millipedes are plant-eaters, while centipedes are fierce **predators**, paralyzing their prey with poison fangs. There are about 11,000 species of centipedes and millipedes.

► A spirobolid millipede (family *Spirobolidae*).

Arachnids

Spiders and their relatives, the scorpions, ticks, and mites, make up the class of animals called arachnids. Like insects, arachnids are invertebrates. Arachnids are also arthropods. There are important differences between insects and arachnids. Arachnids have only two parts to their bodies—the **cephalothorax** (the head and thorax joined together), and a large abdomen. They have four pairs of legs and do not have wings or antennae.

Spider spinners

Spiders (order Araneae) are famous for their silk-making skills. The silk is made inside the spider's body and squeezed out through tiny nozzles, called spinnerets, at its rear. Some spiders weave silk webs to catch their prey. Others are hunters, chasing their prey on the ground. Once the prey is caught, the spider bites and kills it with its poison fangs. There are about 35,000 known species of spiders with perhaps as many as 200,000 still waiting to be discovered.

▲ A huge tropical spider devouring a tree frog.

Sting in the tail

Scorpions (order Scorpionida) have a very distinctive appearance. Like spiders, they have four pairs of legs, and they also have a pair of strong, pincer-like claws, used for grabbing prey. Many scorpions have venomous stings in their tails that they mainly use in self-defense. There are about 800 known species of scorpions.

◄ A yellow desert scorpion (*Butuus quinquestriatus*).

Arachnids get their class name from an Ancient Greek princess, Arachne. Arachne was a skilled weaver and she foolishly boasted that she could weave better than the great goddess, Athena. A contest was held which Arachne won. But Athena was so furious that she turned Arachne into a spider and condemned her to spin forever.

TICKS AND MITES

Ticks and mites (order Acari) are **parasites**, living on other animals and plants, and feeding on their sap, blood, fur, and feathers. Some common mites live on household dust that is mostly made up of flakes of dead human skin! Most are tiny, often less than 0.04 inches long. But they can be deadly, spreading diseases in humans, animals, and food crops. There are about 30,000 known species of ticks and mites.

▲ A wood tick (*Dermacentor andersoni*).

Arachnid classification	
Kingdom:	Animalia (animals)
Phylum:	Arthropoda (arthropods)
Class:	Arachnida (arachnids)
Number of orders:	11
Number of species:	about 75,000

FISH

Fish are vertebrates. There are as many species of fish as all other vertebrates (amphibians, reptiles, birds, and mammals) put together. Fish are **cold-blooded**. They live in water, both fresh and salty, and "breathe" in oxygen through **gills**. Fish are designed for swimming. They have muscular, streamlined bodies often covered in scales, and fins instead of limbs. Fish were the earliest known vertebrates on Earth. The first fish appeared about 515 million years ago.

RUBBERY SKELETONS

Sharks, rays, and skates belong to the group of **cartilaginous** fish (class *Chondrichthyes*). Instead of bone, they have skeletons made of rubbery, flexible **cartilage**. They also have a series of separate gill slits along each side of the body. With its razor-sharp teeth and man-eating reputation, the most famous shark is the great white. But the largest shark is the enormous whale shark that feeds on **plankton**, filtered from the water. It can grow up to 60 feet (18 meters) long, but it is harmless.

▼ Carribbean reef sharks (*Carcharhinus perezi*) are cartilaginous fish.

BONY FISH

More than 95 percent of all fish are bony fish (class Osteichthyes). As their name suggests, bony fish have skeletons made of bone. Their gills are covered by a flap with a single opening at the rear. This group includes fish such as herrings, salmon, angler fish, eels, and carp. Bony fish are found all over the world, from vast oceans to tiny ponds. The longest bony fish is the striking-looking oarfish. It can grow over 30 feet (9 meters) long and looks like a silvery ribbon, with a long, red fin along its back.

HOW FISH BREATHE

Fish use their gills to breathe oxygen dissolved in the water. A fish swims along, opening and closing its mouth. As it opens its mouth, it gulps in water. As it closes its mouth, it pushes the water out again through its gills. As the water passes over the gills, the fish's blood vessels absorb oxygen from the water and release waste carbon dioxide into the water to be pumped out.

DID YOU KNOW ?

Despite its strange S-shaped body, the seahorse is a true fish. It belongs to the same group as sticklebacks and pipefish (order *Gasterosteiformes*). Seahorses are weak, slow swimmers. They use their delicate back fins to help them move along. More often they are seen clinging to seaweed with their sensitive tails.

▲ Seahorses (*Hippocampus hippocampus*) are really fish.

Fish classification	
Kingdom:	Animalia (animals)
Phylum:	Chordata (chordates)
Sub-phylum:	Vertebrata (vertebrates)
Classes:	1. Lampreys and hagfish (jawless fish)
	2. Chondrichthyes (fish with skeletons made of cartilage)
	3. Osteichthyes (fish with skeletons made of bone)
Number of orders:	20
Number of species:	about 24,000 (with about 100 new species discovered every year)

AMPHIBIANS

The ancestors of modern amphibians were the first vertebrates to leave the water to search for food and to live on land. They first appeared on Earth about 370 million years ago. Amphibians are cold-blooded vertebrates. They have smooth, scaleless skin. Their young breathe through gills, like fish. Adult amphibians have lungs, but they also breathe through their skins, which they must keep moist to absorb oxygen properly.

FROGS AND TOADS

Frogs and toads belong to the order Anura. They look very similar but there are several ways of telling them apart. Frogs have smoother skin and longer legs for jumping. Toads may have lumpy warts on their skins and squatter bodies. Most frogs and toads live on or near the ground, and feed on fast-moving prey such as insects and spiders. There are about 3,800 known species of frogs and toads, or anurans, living all over the world. About 20 new species are discovered each year.

► A common frog (order Anura).

NEWTS AND SALAMANDERS

Newts and salamanders belong to the order Urodela or Caudata. They live in the damp undergrowth near water and feed on invertebrates such as slugs, snails, and worms. They have longer bodies and shorter legs than anurans, and long, distinctive tails. When a newt or salamander loses a leg or part of its tail, it can grow a new one. There are about 360 known species of newts and salamanders.

▲ A fire salamander (*Salamandra salamandra*).

CAECILIANS

Caecilians belong to the third order of amphibians, Gymnophiona. Their long, cylindrical shape makes them look more like small snakes. Caecilians do not have legs and are nearly blind. They live in water or burrow in soft earth, feeding on earthworms and other invertebrates. There are about 170 known species of caecilians living in the tropics. Most are about 20 inches (50 centimeters) long, but some reach lengths of 5 feet (1.5 meters).

Amphibian classification	
Kingdom:	Animalia (animals)
Phylum:	Chordata (chordates)
Sub-phylum:	Vertebrata (vertebrates)
Class:	Amphibia (amphibians)
Number of orders:	3
Number of species:	about 4,500

REPTILES

Snakes, lizards, crocodiles, and turtles are all types of reptiles. Reptiles are vertebrates. They are cold-blooded, so they usually live in warm places where the Sun heats their bodies up and makes them active. Reptiles are much better adapted for life on land than amphibians. Their scaly skin protects their bodies and keeps them from drying out, and they lay eggs protected by tough, leathery shells. Some reptiles give birth to live young. There are about 6,500 known species of reptiles, divided into four main orders.

SNAKES AND LIZARDS

With about 6,000 species, snakes and lizards (order *Squamata*) form the largest group of reptiles. Although snakes look very different than lizards, scientists believe they evolved from lizard-like ancestors that had two pairs of legs. Lizards range in size from tiny geckos (family *Gekkonidae*) to the huge Komodo dragon (*Varanus komodoensis*). The longest snake in the world is the reticulated python (*Python reticulatus*) of Southeast Asia, which can grow up to 33 feet (10 meters) long.

▼ A red spitting cobra (*Naja pallida*) coiled around her eggs.

ALLIGATORS AND CROCODILES

Alligators and crocodiles (order *Crocodilia*) are the largest living reptiles. These giants are covered in large, hard scales, strengthened with bone, to form "armor plating." They are well adapted for life in water, using their powerful tails for swimming. Their eyes and nostrils are on top of their heads so that they can lie submerged but still see and breathe. Crocodilians are fierce predators. They drag prey under water and tear it apart with their sharp, pointed teeth.

TURTLES AND TORTOISES

Turtles, tortoises, and terrapins make up the order Chelonia. They have bony shells for protection and beak-like jaws instead of teeth. They live in oceans, rivers, and on land, and feed on plants and small animals. Some turtles and tortoises can live for a very long time. The record for any land animal is 152 years for a Marion's tortoise (*Geochelone gigantea*).

Reptile classification

Kingdom:	Animalia (animals)
Phylum:	Chordata (chordates)
Sub-phylum:	Vertebrata (vertebrates)
Class:	Reptilia (reptiles)
Number of orders:	4 (major)
Number of species:	about 6,500

DID YOU KNOW ?

The tuatara (*Sphenodon punctatus*) is the only living member of an ancient order of reptiles (order *Rhynchocephalia*). Its ancestors appeared about 220 million years ago, before the first dinosaurs. Today, tuatara are only found in New Zealand. Their name comes from a local Maori word meaning "peaks on the back," which refers to the spiky crest growing along the tuatara's back and tail.

▲ A tuatara (*Sphenodon punctatus*).

BIRDS

Birds are **warm-blooded** vertebrates. They are the only animals whose bodies are covered with feathers. Most birds can fly. Birds breathe air through lungs. They have beaks but no teeth, and produce their young by laying eggs with hard shells. Birds are found all over the world, in city centers, steamy rainforests, and at the icy poles. They range in size from the huge African ostrich (Struthio camelus), which stands 6.5 feet (2 meters) tall, to tiny bee hummingbirds (Mellisuga helenae) from Central America, which are no bigger than most butterflies.

PERCHING BIRDS

The largest order of birds is the perching birds (order *Passeriformes*). It includes more than 5,500 species, almost 60 percent of all known birds. Passerines have four toes on their feet, three pointing forwards and one pointing backwards, for gripping on to branches.

► The painted bunting (*Passerina ciris*) is a perching bird.

Bird classification	
Kingdom:	Animalia (animals)
Phylum:	Chordata (chordates)
Sub-phylum:	Vertebrata (vertebrates)
Class:	Aves (birds)
Number of orders:	23
Number of species:	more than 8,500

The first known bird lived on Earth about 150 million years ago. It was given the Latin name *Archaeopteryx*, which means "ancient wings." Fossils found in the 1860s show that it was about the size of a pigeon, with feathers, wings, and a wishbone in its skeleton, like a modern bird. But it also had teeth and a long, bony tail, like a reptile. From creatures like *Archaeopteryx*, scientists have been able to show that birds are the living descendants of dinosaurs.

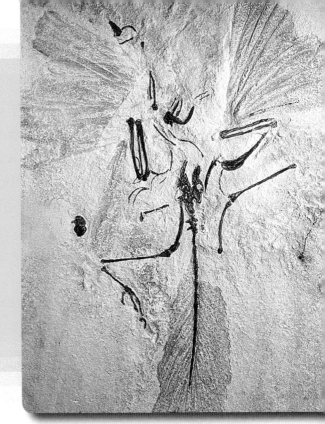

▲ This *Archaeopteryx* fossil was found in Germany.

FLIGHTLESS BIRDS

Some birds, such as ostriches and penguins, have wings but cannot fly. Ostriches (order *Struthioniformes*) are the largest birds in the world. They are too heavy to fly but can run at more than 40 miles (70 kilometers) per hour, faster than a racehorse. Penguins (order *Sphenisciformes*) look clumsy on land but seem to "fly" under water. Using its wings as flippers, the gentoo penguin (*Pygoscelis papua*) can reach speeds of about 25 miles (40 kilometers) per hour, four times faster than the fastest human swimmer.

► The ostrich (*Struthio camelus*) is a flightless bird.

MAMMALS

There are more than 4,000 species of mammals, ranging from huge elephants and whales to tiny bats and shrews. It is the class to which human beings also belong. Mammals are warm-blooded vertebrates that breathe air using lungs. They all suckle their young on milk and are the only animals that produce milk. They also care for their young until they are old enough to fend for themselves. Mammals are the only animals with ear flaps to channel sound down into their ears.

MARSUPIALS

Marsupials (order *Marsupiala*) are mammals that usually have pouches. They include kangaroos, koalas, and wombats. Their newborn young are very tiny and weak. After birth, they crawl into their mother's pouch where they feed on milk and grow.

MONOTREMES

Three species of mammals—the duck-billed platypus, the long-beaked echidna and the short-beaked echidna—belong to the order Monotremata. Monotremes are mammals that lay eggs. A female duck-billed platypus (*Ornithorhynchus anatinus*) lays her soft eggs in a riverbank tunnel. When the young hatch, she nurses them like other mammals.

▲ Kangaroos are marsupials.

Mammal classification	
Kingdom:	Animalia (animals)
Phylum:	Chordata (chordates)
Sub-phylum:	Vertebrata (vertebrates)
Class:	Mammalia (mammals)
Sub-classes:	1 Prototheria (egg-laying)
	2 Theria (do not lay eggs)
Infra-classes:	1 Eutheria (**placental**)
	2 Metatheria (non-placental)
Number of orders:	19
Number of species:	more than 4,000

Mammal Orders

Order	Examples	No. of species
Artiodacytyla	Camels, pigs, cattle	about 180
Carnivora	Cats, bears, dogs	about 250
Cetacea	Whales, dolphins	72
Chiroptera	Bats	about 800
Dermoptera	Flying lemurs	2
Edentata	Anteaters, sloths	29
Hyracoidea	Hyraxes	about 6
Insectivora	Moles, shrews	about 350
Lagomorpha	Rabbits, hares	about 60
Marsupiala	Kangaroos, koalas	about 275
Monotremata	Platypus, spiny anteater	3
Perissodactyla	Tapirs, rhinos, horses	15
Pholidota	Pangolins	7
Pinnipedia	Seals, sea lions, walrus	34
Primates	Lemurs, monkeys, humans	about 200
Proboscidea	Elephants	2
Rodentia	Mice, porcupines, beavers	about 1750
Sirenia	Dugongs, manatees	4
Tubulidentata	Aardvark	1

DID YOU KNOW ?

The aardvark (*Orycteropus afer*) is the only living member of its order (*Tubulidendata*). This unusual ant-eating mammal lives in the **grasslands** of Africa. Its body is specialized for burrowing after its food, with long, spade-shaped claws and powerful back legs. Instead of running away from enemies, it digs a hole and hides. As it digs, it folds back its ears and closes its nostrils to keep out the soil.

▲ An aardvark (*Orycteropus afer*).

MORE MAMMALS

Most mammals are placental mammals. Their babies grow inside their mothers' bodies until they are fully formed. They receive nourishment from their mother through her placenta, and when they are born, they look like smaller versions of their parents. Placental mammals include whales, bats, and human beings.

FLYING MAMMALS

Bats (order *Chiroptera*) make up nearly a quarter of all mammal species. Bats are the only mammals that can truly fly, although some mammals can glide. The name Chiroptera is Latin for "hand-wings." This is because a bat's wings have evolved from its hands and arms. Its finger bones are very long, with leathery skin stretched between them, leaving the thumb free. The wings are also attached to the bat's back legs and tail. There are two main groups of bats—large fruit bats, or flying foxes, and smaller insect-eaters.

▲ Geoffroy's long-nosed bat (*Anoura geoffroyi*).

DID YOU KNOW ?

The African elephant (*Loxodonta africana*) is the world's largest living land mammal. An adult bull (male) elephant can weigh more than 5 tons and stand 10 feet (3 meters) tall. Incredibly, their closest mammal relative is believed to be the rabbit-sized hyrax (order Hyracoidea). They are thought to have originated from the same mammal group some 55 million years ago.

► Cape hyraxes (*Procavia capensis*).

SEA MAMMALS

There are about 120 species of sea mammals, belonging to three orders—Cetacea (whales and dolphins), Pinnipedia (seals, sea lions, and walruses) and Sirenia (dugongs and manatees). Sea mammals include the gigantic blue whale, the largest mammal that has ever lived. Blue whales (*Balaenoptera musculus*) can weigh 130 tons and grow more than 100 feet (30 meters) long.

HUMAN MAMMALS

Human beings (*Homo sapiens*) belong to the order of primates. There are about 200 species of primates, divided into two groups. The anthropoids include apes (chimpanzees, gorillas, orangutans, and gibbons), monkeys, and humans. The prosimians include bush babies and lemurs. Humans are very closely related to apes. Gorillas and chimpanzees are more closely related to us than they are to orangutans.

▲ Young chimpanzees (*Pan troglodytes*).

Human classification	
Kingdom:	Animalia (animals)
Phylum:	Chordata (chordates)
Sub-phylum:	Vertebrata (vertebrates)
Class:	Mammalia (mammals)
Sub-class:	Eutheria (placental)
Order:	Primates (primates)
Family:	Hominidae (homonids)
Species:	*Homo sapiens* (humans)

GLOSSARY

abdomen end part of an insect's or arachnid's body

algae very simple plants found in salt and fresh water

antennae feeler-like sense organs on an insect's head. They are used for touching, sensing changes in temperature, and detecting tastes and smells.

cartilage rubbery, flexible tissue that, instead of bone, makes up the skeletons of fish such as sharks

cartilaginous made of cartilage

cellulose tough material that makes the fibers found in plant cell walls

cephalothorax front part of an arachnid's body, made up of the head and thorax joined together

chlorophyll green pigment (coloring) found inside plant cells. It absorbs energy from sunlight for use in photosynthesis.

chordate organism that, at some time in its life, has a stiff, skeletal rod of cells running along and supporting its spinal cord

cold-blooded animals, such as fish, amphibians, and reptiles, that cannot control their own body temperature. They rely on the weather to warm them up or cool them down.

compound eyes special eyes of many insects. Each eye is made up of hundreds of tiny, individual lenses.

deciduous trees and plants that regularly shed their leaves

exoskeleton tough, outer coat or shell of invertebrates such as insects or crabs. It protects and supports their soft bodies.

gill thin, feathery organ that a fish uses for breathing in oxygen from the water

grassland large, open, flat area covered in grasses and low bushes. Grasslands cover about a quarter of the land on Earth.

invertebrate animal that does not have a backbone or hard skeleton inside its body

Latin language originally spoken in Ancient Rome. Many modern languages are based on Latin. It is the language used in science to name living things.

nucleus rounded structure inside a cell. It is the cell's control center, regulating everything that happens inside the cell.

organ group of different tissues in a living thing's body. A human's heart and lungs are examples of organs.

organism scientific word for a living thing

organ system group of organs working together in a living thing's body. A person's digestive system is an organ system. It uses various organs, such as the stomach and intestines.

ovule female sex cell of a flowering plant or conifer. After fertilization, ovules become seeds.

parasite plant or animal that lives on or in another plant or animal and gets all its food from them

photosynthesis process by which green plants make food from carbon dioxide and water, using energy from sunlight absorbed by their chlorophyll

placental placental mammals are those whose young develop inside their mothers' bodies until they are fully formed

plankton tiny plants and animals that live in water and provide food for many other animals

pollen tiny grains that contain the male sex cells of flowering plants and conifers

pollination transfer of pollen from a male flower to a female flower or from the male part of a flower to the female part so that fertilization can happen

predators animals that hunt and kill other animals for food

prey animals that are hunted and eaten by other animals

species group of organisms that are grouped together because they have similar features and can breed with each other

spore tiny, dust-like speck produced by fungi and many non-flowering plants. Spores grow into new plants.

taxonomy the way in which living things are divided into groups, based on the features they have in common. This makes them easier to identify and study. It is also called classification.

thorax middle part of an insect's body bearing the legs and wings

tissue group of cells in a living thing's body that have a special job to do. Bones and muscle are types of tissues.

tube feet tiny, tube-like tentacles, which starfish and other echinoderms have. They use them for breathing, moving, and grasping food.

vascular tissue system of tubes, called xylem and phloem, inside a plant that carries water and food around

vein part of a plant's vascular tissue. Veins also help to strengthen a plant's leaves and support them to give them their shape.

vertebrae interlinked bones in a vertebrate's backbone

vertebrate animal with a backbone and skeleton inside its body. Fish, amphibians, reptiles, birds, and mammals are all vertebrates.

warm-blooded animals that can control their own body temperature so that it stays the same whatever the weather outside. This allows them to be active in the heat or cold.

FIND OUT MORE

Internet research

You can find out more about classification on the Internet. Use a search engine such as www.google.com or www.yahooligans.com to search for information. A search for "classification" will bring back lots of results but it may be difficult to find the information you want. Try refining your search to look for some of the specific animals, plants, or ideas mentioned in this book, such as "invertebrates," "conifers," or "insect classification."

More books to read

Classifying Living Things (series) Chicago: Heinemann, 2004.

Ganeri, Anita. *Animal Groupings*. New York: Chelsea House, 2004.

INDEX